CUMBRIA LIBRARY SERVICES

COUNTY COUNCIL
This book is due to be returned on or before the last date above. It may be renewed by personal application, post or telephone, if not in demand.

C.L.18

GHOSTS

John Fuller

Chatto & Windus
LONDON

Published by Chatto & Windus 2004

2 4 6 8 10 9 7 5 3 1

Copyright © John Fuller 2004

John Fuller has asserted his right under the Copyright, Designs
and Patents Act 1988 to be identified as the author of this work

First published in Great Britain in 2004 by
Chatto & Windus
Random House, 20 Vauxhall Bridge Road,
London SW1V 2SA

Random House Australia (Pty) Limited
20 Alfred Street, Milsons Point, Sydney,
New South Wales 2061, Australia

Random House New Zealand Limited
18 Poland Road, Glenfield,
Auckland 10, New Zealand

Random House (Pty) Limited
Endulini, 5A Jubilee Road, Parktown 2193, South Africa

The Random House Group Limited Reg. No. 954009
www.randomhouse.co.uk

A CIP catalogue record for this book
is available from the British Library

ISBN 0 7011 7740 3

recyclable p   rests;
the man   al

Typ

ACKNOWLEDGEMENTS

Grateful acknowledgments are made to the following, in which some of these poems first appeared: *Agenda*, *Areté*, *Essays in Criticism*, Grand Phoenix Press (Nîmes), *Guardian*, *London Magazine*, *London Review of Books*, *Magdalen College Record*, *Oxford Magazine*, *Oxford Poetry*, *Poetry Nation Review*, *Thumbscrew*, *Times Literary Supplement*.

CONTENTS

GHOSTS

The fire, springing to wispish life
On yesterday's raked coals, breaks out
Into its yellow authentic shapes.

The radio is building a library,
Discussing 'big-boned' minuets
Over a second breakfast tea.

Rain for the moment forbids a walk.
The hillside grasses flatten. Sheep
Graze into the frame of the window.

This, then, is the moment to
Review the images I woke with:
Human shapes with the spirit gone.

Dreams already broken when
I folded your nightdress, understanding
That cartoon symbol of the departed.

The swooping spook that certain cupboards
And staircases allow to haunt
With resentment and unfinished business.

Itself insubstantial, it
Invests sleeves with empty gestures,
Deep hems with a power to float.

But mostly troubles us with simple
Melancholy, hugging its own
Knee-hump before a fading fire

Like the girl who was a woman
Before she was old enough to look
Further than her day of pain.

2

Is it possible? Suddenly arms
And hair in the dark passageway,
A touch, and a draught of cold air?

Or the rumour of shadows against lit windows
In empty cottages on a mountain
Where night and the rain are masterful?

We can only believe in what we believe
To have been absolutely worthy
Of being somehow recoverable.

Not ourselves, certainly, existing
Nowhere but in the imagining
Of such imagining and capture.

We think of those whom we still owe
Some gesture, those we would have liked
To know, those we knew best of all.

Or is it that we have translated
Our unique consciousness into
A wish to persist and to survive?

Perhaps we are both victim and visitant,
Willing and sensuous in both roles,
Willing and fearful, like a lover?

These are chairs where the dead have suddenly
Sat bolt upright in the realisation
At once of presence and transience.

These are the shadowed ceilings where
Dreams ceased at an unfamiliar
Noise and speculation began.

These are the unoiled doors opening
On to rooms where a new consciousness
Of brief tenure sharpened the shapes

Of furniture that changed tense,
Where time that was neither night nor morning
Clung to objects that were going nowhere.

It hardly matters who felt these things,
For they are what we know we share.
The connection itself becomes the ghost.

3

And then I remembered figures falling
Willingly, escaping death
Only by freely postponing it

To take a few more breaths of their
Planet's precious gases, high-risk
Commodity eighty floors up.

And they were neither graceful nor clumsy.
They were neither living nor dead.
For this moment they lost their names.

For this moment, turning as if
Recumbent, one leg crooked as if
Finding comfort in sleeplessness,

They became simply the transient forms
Of their deliverance from being:
Handlocked divers, impossible stars.

They were arms and legs and trousers,
Already emptied, already ghosts.
They had overstayed their body's welcome.

Their city had betrayed them. Alive
Still in our sleep, they are like the damned
Spilling from an altarpiece.

Somewhere there is always ash
That has no glow or stirring in it.
Only a wind, lifting its surface.

A wind that buckets and yells across
These hills, beyond the parish, beyond
The oceans, all around the globe,

And has no notion what it can
Be chasing, or why, except that they are
Something like our vagrant thoughts,

That live in one place for a while,
And it blows them onwards and is their
Tormentor, deafening our dreams.

PRESCIENCE

To mourn throughout your life
That unknown day when you
Wake up for the last time
Is quite impossible.
It will arrive when it
Decides to, and will not
Be denied, though it be
Painful and unannounced.

Still, we toy with this thought
And find the resonance
Attractive to our sense
Of the deep recklessness
Of all physical hopes
Which nonetheless rely
On celebration and
Calendar calculations.

No candles on a cake,
Unless a countback from
Your theoretical
Threescore-and-ten might serve.
No congratulations,
Since all you have achieved
Is a noted dwindling.
What a licence for gloom!

No presents: far better
A disburdening of
All earthly possessions,
A practised letting go.
And yet the unseen guests
At the non-existent
Party expect some words.
It is that kind of day.

Take the example of
Virginia Woolf, who
In 1941
Walked into the Ouse on
The 28th of March,
Thus forever putting
From her like a locked door
The fear of going mad.

On that very same day
A dozen years before,
With deathday prescience
She opened her journal
And her pen sailed over
The calm flowing of the
Page: 'I met Nessa in
Tottenham Court Road this

Afternoon, both of us
Sunk fathoms deep in that
Wash of reflection in
Which we both swim about.'
And then, with precision,
Wrote: 'Only in myself . . .
Forever bubbles this
Impetuous torrent.'

She continued thus in
1929: 'I
Feel on the verge of some
Strenuous adventure.'
In 1930 (though
She was writing about
Her novel *The Waves*): 'How
To end . . . I do not know.'

The following year her
Nib broke the surface of
The ink: 'Arnold Bennett
Died last night' were its words.
In 1935:
'Spring triumphant.' And in
1937:
'I shall lapse into dreams.'

These were deathday speeches:
Gracious, though in places
Troubled; prophetic, though
Never balefully so.
Whatever you are heard
To say on your deathday
You may be sure that it
Will hardly be noticed.

In fact, no one will be
There to wish you many
Unhappy returns; no
Cards clatter through your box.
But make no mistake. Death
Will come one day, smiling,
With that shape you must guess:
The stone in his pocket.

FLEA MARKET

Place de Jeu de Balle, Brussels

And there will never be a time
When we will go down in the darkness,
Waiting until the platform clears

To open the stiff doors of the last tram
To Silence, lifting our failing feet
And unwillingly replacing them

Until we reach that square of dispersals,
To see our own lives laid out
On the cobbles for the scavengers.

We will never weep to see our pathetic
Trophies laid out on newspaper,
Turned over by the toe of profit

Or still heaped in their cartons of haulage
Where nothing is thought to be beautiful
That cannot survive its ownership.

The things we liked are like the things
We did, kept by us and remembered,
But imperfect to the judicious eye.

Weaknesses like photographs,
Faces instinctively lifted towards
A supposed immortality.

Wounded plates preserved in the uniform
Of their fortunate brothers, loved music
Cheapened by pencil and blackened corners.

The things that are only what they pretend
To be for as long as one pays them attention:
Papers flowers, magazine parts.

Objects that tease by confusing the appetites:
The mammary jelly-mould, the mannekin
Corkscrew, the can-can casse-noisette.

The trophies from foreign shores and occasions:
The coloured sand, the Exhibition
Mug, the aluminium amulet.

What has always been said is also
True: you can't take it with you.
So let us establish a useful countdown

Like eating the contents of the fridge
Before departure, to the last undated
Egg, saved rice and dwindled caper.

Such were a satisfying meal,
Though frugal, and appropriate
To the condemned prisoners we are.

All these objects that we believe
Define us: they ache already with
Our love, and their forgottenness.

DIFFERENT PLACES

The world is always beginning somewhere,
Springing again to life in rooms
Lost for a time in darkness.
Look: the pad of your finger presses
The affirming plastic, placed in the corner
Of its white wall like a postage stamp,
And the room is suddenly sheepishly lit,
Encouraging talk and smiling, like
A theatre during the interval.

Decision, motion, intention: all
These we are reminded of
By the room's connected distances.
But then to enter and enjoy
Must be to leave the somewhere else
That you inevitably were
To its equivalence of darkness,
For despite our wishes, we are never
In more than one place at a time.

Proposal: to turn unthinking habit
Into the first superb performance
Of something you have long rehearsed,
To make a lively parade of waking
Wherever we happen to find ourselves
And to know that now is always different
And so to bless hot water stirring
In the veins of the house, the practical talking
Of a child who has forgotten his nightmares

And other distant sounds: the thud
Of a neighbour's door, the bronchial revving
From the street of someone's early start,
And nearer: the breath still passing
Above or below the palate, a tide

That laps the hull of destination
In the almost audible warmth of the skull,
The one place where you always are,
The steady engine-room of the heart.

AIR RAID

Autumn's a brute. The trees
Raise arms to ward off blows,
Twisting from side to side.

There's nowhere they can hide.
How unsuspecting once
They struck their attitudes

Of poise and lift, blessing
The bounty of the light,
Alive to their very tips!

These broken limbs are like
A retribution exacted
For their vain need of transcendence:

Uplifted wrists scattered,
Old elbows dangling
In streams, shoulders smashed.

The punishment is random:
The vulnerable birch
Ignored, the sturdy ash

Split to the bole, and twenty
Oaks picked out in the wood,
Hoping to be unnoticed.

You, and you, and you,
Yes, and you! Here
And there, where the wind passed.

Lying against the hill
The trees seem merely tired,
Glad to have given up.

Some reeling at an angle
With a clod of stones and roots
That might bob them back like a toy.

Some still carrying parts
Of themselves, the injuries matching,
Splintered stumps and sockets.

Some defeated by a gust,
Top heavy with ivy.
Throttled, they soon gave up.

Some with their fury of leaves
Crushed into the grass,
Stunned, unlikely to stir.

What will we do with them?
No forgetting the place
That they had made their own.

No concealment of loss,
No mending of wounds like these,
No heaving to the vertical.

No averting the eye
From damage. But in
The stillness, the saws are busy.

FINAL MOVES

In Memory of Dirk ter Haar

Your last moves are postmarked
A week before your breathing
Took its turn for the worst

And your mind, with all the skills
And data of a lifetime,
Was filed away, and the key lost.

And I, being out of the country,
Catch up with both events
A month later, on the same day.

Three weeks are nothing much
When misspent, but are here
A strange survival, unique

And unknown to anyone,
Neither to you, mourned,
Nor to me in my pleasures.

This play of thought upon
The pure and possible
Issues in the intercourse

Of a friendly aggression,
Decisiveness sealed with a stamp
And the launch of the envelope

Which can, at a refolding
Of the card, show the either address
Of colleagues who only speak

In a precise abstraction
From the world and its clumsy hopes,
Attempting the play of perfection.

What do we have here?
In Game A, your liberation
From my too-early assault

Upon your cautious Najdorf
Gives you an open file
Against my extra pawn

And with a typical calm
Your Kg8 prepares
For a more dogged defence.

In Game B, Your Ng5
Ignores my reckless queenside
Rampage, pretending it is nothing,

Cunningly condoning my desire
To devour with Na2
Your a-pawn or win the exchange.

Or both. But if I do,
You have Qf1! and counterplay
Against my sparse kingside.

Calm and cunning: your twin
Virtues in this volatile
Battle of locked wills

Whose code of advance and withdrawal
Over its limited landscape
Attempts to locate the Correct,

That fallible intrusion
Of human discipline into
The study of natural things.

For seven months I'd stared
At this red card where the notation
Of your forays required attention

But in your last week of waiting
I was lying in entire ignorance
By a chessless southern sea.

For that week, your body
Was still busy at its being,
Intent on its earthly concerns.

Your moves were simply the latest,
Not yet the last, in a series
Senseless without conclusion.

They lived in a limbo of suspense,
Where daily you might have expected
The envelope's return

But soon were consigned to despair,
The frustration of mental events
That now have nowhere to return to

And remain, like the questions
We ask of life itself,
Exact, but unanswerable.

Because you loved this game
I ponder my replies
And imagine your own responses.

But there is a limited point
In such a belated search,
For sorrow wins no advantage.

And after all, we know
That our own biographies,
With all their imagination,

Whether long-planned, or lightly
Extemporised, can never
Contain our final move.

DATES

11 February 2002

Today my father would be 90
But for the final capitulation
Of his familar presence in space
Occurring in 1991,
A date of digital chiasmus
Not very frequently encountered.

An early example comes to mind,
Suggesting an appropriate symbolism:
1111, when al-Ghazali,
The greatest Muslim after Muhammad,
Finally withdrew from the world
He so tentatively lived in.

The date, whichever way you look
At it, is a golden palisade
Between the other world and this.
Are these representations
Our occasional destiny?
And was this true of my father's death?

At the time, after a length
Of trouble, I remember only
The suspended moment of letting go:
From the deep transfixion of his sleep
And uncertain breathing, the flicker across
His face, a little snarl in death.

But now the year in its perfect shape
Seems ironic: a couple with hung
Heads standing between guards.
Till now, these palindromic dates
Have arrived at intervals beyond
Our lifespan: 110 years.

And so the previous one goes back
To 1881, before
Brookville Road in Fulham
Where his grandmother was set up
By her mysterious furrier, and bore him
Minnie and Leopold, aunt and father.

That year's icon is appropriate:
Two babies together within
The walls of their fatherless house.
But now already the year folds back
Upon itself. Its shape is
Mirrored in the line between

The century and our distance from it,
Between the hardly changing and
The changed, the digits of our scope.
The icon? Neither death nor birth,
More like a marriage: two rings, and we
Kneeling with lowered heads beside them.

SNAP, CRACKLE, POP

Noise from a joint has three sources,
Three conditions, three troubles:
Arthritis, tendon flick
And gas bubbles.

Knee-bends were once a healthy sign
Of the physical life we seek.
We kept a strict account
Of every creak.

As language hides in gorgeous robes
Our superstition, like a druid,
The knee is a bag of cartilage
Filled with fluid.

This little model of your body
Is all that you'd expect,
Snapping to attention when
You genuflect.

The reason is the reduced pressure:
Gas in the blood expands
When the ligaments stretch
Like elastic bands.

Every reason, then, to stay upright
Like the citizen you carelessly claim
To be of the Eternal City
In intention and name.

For myself, I'd rather be pure spirit,
With a love that is boundless
Beyond the grating of surfaces,
Painless and soundless.

Torture is the extremest proof of feeling
In bodies that have known their time.
Love has been vigilance, and regret.
Now it is kneeling.

Obeisance is not obedience.
To bow is not to obey.
We would still like to will our conditions,
To buy but not to pay.

There will be ways enough of folding up
Our bodily ration less ridiculous
Than this, no doubt, when God
Takes down our particulars.

THE PHILOSOPHER KING

The arms of chairs appear
To have ideas about
How we should sit in them.

They want us to grasp each end
With whitened knuckles like
A stage Plantagenet,

To lean forward, musing,
Slightly to one side,
One elbow raised behind us

In a grave posture of judgement,
Of deliberative wisdom,
A finger stroking the lip.

But there's no one in front of us,
No slave, no supplicant,
No arrogant adviser.

Thumb moves upon the grain,
Eyes cast about the room,
Head leans gently back.

But still the arms of the chair
Remind us of a duty
To reach into our thoughts.

If our fingers touch each other,
Our forearms complete a diamond
For the cat to jump into.

If we narrow our elbows
And lower them to our sides,
We feel strangely diminished.

We shrink into the chair
As a victim shrinks, resigned
To execution or teasing.

In fact, the roles are reversed
And the philosopher king
Is almost confined to a corpse.

Quick then: our royal proposals
Must launch a brilliant era
Of unarguable truth

Before we fall back upon
Protest or complaint,
Or lachrymose last-words.

HAPPY

for Emily

I

The two hundred and six most difficult pieces
And all the missing lights are now assembled,
Proving at last the whole triumphant thesis
That what in sonar otherness resembled
A fleshly anagram is now a shape
Made manifest, a clue now finally
Its satisfying reason, sole to nape,
Tree of the spine and apple of the knee.

This warm celebrity tells us a thing
Or two, or three: when answers must be right,
How art is always public, and how mothers
Must give much more than artists when they bring
Their concept of the human to the light.
Why we are most ourselves becoming others

Parted, and yet not parted. Nowhere to hide
But everywhere. This is the paradox
Of being where he never was, outside
Or inside, little spring of the living box,
Folded mechanism of surprise.
So the immediate applause is his,
Appearing now before our very eyes.
No wonder that he got here: here he is.

And yet dependent still, and still at rest
He's beached like Crusoe, damp upon your breast
As though the struggle of his voyage meant
Only to make this resting-place the same
Safe home, or like the object of a game,
Where touching, he remains in touch, content.

3

There is a mystery in these earliest days.
They have an air of aftermath, amounting
To time suspended, out of your daily ways.
They don't belong with those that you were counting.
Nor with the future of a life that seems
For now to be content with breathing well.
You wake to them as children long for dreams
Where all their wishes find a working spell.

And yet the day itself is sacred now
And will be much remembered. Think of how
The run-up to it so obsessed you, though
The date was still unknown. In years to come
The countdown will be his, and his the sum
Of blazing birthdays that will see him grow.

4

What was the face before it was assigned
These wild expressions that betray the will?
Where was the will itself? And where the mind?
We think the future is a shape to fill,
A cheque to write, a life to give a name,
As though not knowing it is like our knowing
All that we do know, really just the same
But like a debt with only interest owing.

And so our hope fulfilled is unaffected
In many ways by being long expected.
How strange it seems! For though we find the traces
Here and there of features we know well,
It is his own, a story he can tell
Over and over, his face among our faces.

5

His season opens like an opening door.
Outside the window trees bear on their arms
New leaves like napkins stiffly folded for
The banquet of the summer. On his palms
Are similar fresh creases, and like leaves
His fingers are unfolding. Blossoms fall.
The street resumes its life: a push-bike weaves
Its idle circles, joggers hold up a wall.

And from above come sounds of that event
He celebrates with arias of content,
His waking. This is the world that he must bless,
For you who make him happy in it know
That he could only be so, truly so,
In certainty of your own happiness.

6

This little man's the robber of your sleep,
Spending his own brown eyes like currency
Where everything is ruinously cheap
And what he sees a second time is free.
He wakes to look, and he will wake you too
To look with him. The more he looks, the more
You look as well, and often, looking through
His eyes, you see things never seen before.

Yourself included. Look at that colour, full
To the pupils, like two buttons ready to pull
You to him, fastening him to your gaze.
Round as the unscrewed bottle of brown ink
Or two Welsh teapots touching above the sink,
A welcome in their bellied umber glaze.

That sound of his! Not quite an exhalation
Defining joy, nor yet a breathing-in
That strangely turns into an exclamation.
Something between a shudder and a grin
That borrows some of the still air around him
And with a dipping head that makes it dance
Takes it into his throat, which to astound him
Returns it as a kind of utterance.

Is this how language starts, by accident?
Or did he choose the sound for what he meant?
And how does meaning know it has that choice?
He makes the sound again, and often. Surely
Feeling has found a form, and gently, purely,
Recklessly, has turned into his voice.

8

There comes into his face, as though across
A planet movement of the wind or tides,
A gathering, a being at a loss,
A troubling of the sky when the moon glides
From its concealing clouds, a realising
Of some required address, the resolution
Of an enquiry of his own devising,
A play of muscle that is its solution.

It causes something like itself to be
The bright occasion of becoming the
Convincing model of the shape it takes.
Another face, of course! And he relates
Its smile to some idea he imitates,
Since making faces is the game he makes.

9

And now he hauls himself up to your knee
As if a couple of feet makes any clearer
Those things he knows he can already see,
As if a room's horizon could be nearer.
Extended on his tummy like a seal,
He chirps, and gropes for purchase with his toes.
He cranes his neck, and then decides to feel
The carpet with his forehead, tongue and nose.

In either posture (elevated, prone)
He lets you know that he is on his own.
The effort is laborious and full-frontal.
Standing will follow from the being tall;
From being extended he will learn to crawl.
Viva the vertical! Hey, horizontal!

Where do the old gods go when they retire?
When velvet ropes define museum spaces
In front of obelisks once crowned by fire?
When names are unremembered, and their faces?
Not that they do not have their worshippers.
They do. Those who still see them, and who gaze
At them with interest, and unlike us
Count their own wisdom not in years but days.

We recognise this worship in his eyes
By something in their colour, depth and size,
Like windows on to lawns where if you waited
Long enough you might expect to see
The gods happy again, and quietly
Pottering in the garden they created.

THE EMPEROR FELIX

In the first year of his reign
The Emperor Felix composed
His famous hymn to the light.

Sought: the ready blessing of
His immediate ancestor
To rise from the couch of the night.

In the second year of his reign
The Emperor Felix visited
The four corners of his empire.

Measured: the heights and surfaces,
The location of useful resources,
The paces of pilgrimage.

In the third year of his reign
Figs were placed before him,
And bread, and milk and honey.

Favours: whimsical largesse
To the tasters of his food
And the two great cats acknowledged.

In the fourth year of his reign
His activity was marked,
The significant works begun.

Ordered: the transport of gravel,
Circulation of the terraces,
Enumeration of flora.

Historians are uncertain
About the middle years
Of this illustrious reign.

Legend proposes the descent
Of an all-encompassing slumber,
A cessation of enquiry.

How then to account for
The beating of the stone drum
And the heroic investigation

Of that murmuring surface
Which second by second betrays
Its resistance to the horizontal?

How may we accommodate
The richly varied achievements,
The cautious calculations,

The staggering collection
Of objects whose precise use
Is to this day uncertain?

During his reign his shadow
Fell in every direction.
He was tireless, and worshipped.

He was carried everywhere
At his pleasure, his demands
Promptly acceded to.

Long ago we abandoned
Our gods, in disbelief.
But him we still believe in.

TWO ROADS

The future man trots gamely
Into the first definable
Prospects of his life
No further than a flower
Or where the cat was
Or a familiar voice.

But then, as time goes on,
Horizons hold no fear.
The known is not enough.
The whole world exists
To be stumbled through
With whatever sprawling, or sitting.

And off again at a pace
That gives no sign of faltering
Or guessing at resting-places
But aims to cover the ground,
That route between Now and Now
Which is a continued delight.

Our own tired road is shorter,
Anchored as it is to Then,
Uncertain, as ever, of When.

EXCITEMENT

We should give thanks to be living with infants.
They wake so early that it is still
Yesterday, and the house is still.

Their talking brings us many times
Back from the welcoming slope of sleep.
We really would rather be asleep.

But soon they and the wooden crocodile
Are eating cereal and toast and Marmite
And their faces wear moustaches of Marmite.

Their day proceeds with demonstrations
Of studio skills: potato stars
And green hands, and prints of stars.

Sonar detection of the maternal
Force reassures the monsters
That they are not exclusively monsters

And hunger is appeased both
By frightened mice and frequent biscuits,
With preference given to the biscuits.

So it goes on, and what they remind
Us of is the fact that every day,
Though taking the shape of the previous day,

Is nonetheless a unique theatre
Both for familiar events
And less familiar events.

We are restored to the excitement
Of getting on with the business of living
Our lives and simply enjoying living

For there comes a time when we no longer
Wish we could go on sleeping for ever,
Because we are asleep for ever.

GREAT-GRANDFATHER

Released at last from their own interests,
The generations pounce and leapfrog,
Having nothing better to do

Than to question their posterity
Or to rock unsteadily on stones
Across the wet places of nostalgia.

We take adjacent generations
Much for granted. Born from them
Or giving birth to them is enough.

We take them much like draughtsmen
To reach the vantage of our vision:
The daughter's son, the mother's father.

Or further, the mother's grandfather,
The grandfather's grandfather, squares
Beyond capture, where vaulting stumbles.

These are the unimaginable
Places where the game changes
And the living blood laps at its borders.

The dear ones who would love us if
They could, and who have never touched us,
Are troubled no longer by their progeny.

We have their jokes and illnesses,
Little rules by which our game
Continues to be understood,

But their lives and faces are motionless.
How shall we ever know them? How
Shall we cry across that absolute

That keeps them from us? For only we
Can hold out our hands in hope
Of grasping something more than shadow.

As my grandson said of my dead father:
'Well, when he's finished being dead,
We'll go to see him then.'

COMPENSATIONS

We wake to our finer perceptions
Or at least with the most precise
And lie in wonder at them.

We catch them emerging fresh
From the seed-bed of our dreams
Waiting to sprout into life.

What a pity it is
That however true in essence
Their terms make little sense.

They shrivel and dry in the light
Of our eager attention,
Ready to be forgotten.

Why should German phonemes
Be textually embodied
In tiny slivers of bacon?

My jocular explanation
That I'm a vegetarian
Is entirely unconvincing.

It must be a linguistic
Code, or some classification
Like knots or chromosomes.

Am I too confident
In understanding such things?
I look at my lecture in dismay

While the others in low tunes
Are talking with reason and purpose
In ways impossible to follow.

My labelling the thing
(Brilliantly) 'half-mauve'
And even 'quarter-mauve'

('Morve' it was, not 'mowve',
As being the little-known
Correct pronunciation)

Was a compensating triumph,
And so I pursued the thought:
'Quarter-mauve/coffee!'

Delighted that I had noted
The blind elusive mauve
Quality of coffee.

These pedantic evasions
Are symbols of real guilt
At our terrible failings,

Of our retreat to podiums
Of self-esteem, to pillows
Of sobbing self-disgust.

Our waking catches us out,
Frozen in attitudes
Of breathtaking imposture.

And soon we have forgotten
Whatever sense we had
Of what it was all about.

Just as Susan, with a smile,
Goes on drinking quarter-
Mauve and Maas as though

This was a common thing,
Something that everyone does
Every day of their lives.

HORIZONS

There is a fresh romance
In the very edge of sight:
What is the view from that sail
That is our view? Looking
Onwards, no doubt, at something
We can't begin to guess at.

Or maybe looking back
At us? Are we a horizon?
And if *we* look the other way?
There are no limits to mystery.
It eludes our focus,
And begins to map the globe.

INSECTS

These sun-spirits please themselves
And please us, not least by being
Busy at what they are about:
The haste of gossamer, lacing
Side-mirror to window
Before the engine cools.
The dragonfly unwinding
In elastic uncertainty,
Hovering above a pool.
And this bird-headed thing
Whirring from its waist,
Sipping the mimosa.

I see how we could have believed
In sylphs and goblins, posting
To the four corners of the air
And ministering to the sleight
Of seasons, the disappearance
Of the sustaining day.
For insects have this sense
Of catching time on the wing
And outwitting it, and us.
They have surely come from somewhere
And are off again without
Pause, steady of purpose.

Though for the second that we see them
They behave like idiots,
Shame-faced, shambolic:
The fly wrings its hands,
Staring into mid-distance.
The bee falls from its flower.
Mostly the moth, clattering
At lamps, drowning in wax,
Fails fully to impress,

Encountered in the morning,
Still, on the bathroom wall,
A bivouac in snow,
The high heroics forgotten,
Stranded between peaks
Of impossible enlarging flight.

Perhaps it is this failure
That gives us the licence to
Refigure them as fairies,
Commanding in their whims
And bracing transformations,
One step ahead of time.
But touchingly clumsy, too,
As we are clumsy. Feckless,
Changeable, mistaken.
Shakespeare's Ariel knew
The sweetness of the cowslip
But wanted to be all spirit.
And Disney's winged nymphet
Going down on a daffodil
Or lazily stringing dew
Has the air of choosing a flavour
Or an accidental jewel
That reflects credit on her.

It is we humans who wish
To be admired, to be free,
When we know we are powerless.
We are so aware of alternatives
That we invent the gift of magic
Which lightly ignores them.
We would love to be so small
As barely to be seen, to fly
And to utterly change our shape.

This would be a fine distinction
To compensate for life's brevity
And its insignificance.

AJ 845418

for Alexandre Pireddu

Once again the rubber craft
Is wheeled to the water over the stones
That wear their morning colours still:

Rose, violet, charcoal, fawn,
Distinctions that the sun will kindle
To the indiscriminate whiteness of noon

When your father, grandfather and uncles
Will sit beneath the parasol,
Elbows on knees, to gut the catch.

And shall we live to see you join them?
To limber down the path under the hedge,
To push off from the rock with an oar?

To sit and talk of this and that
In the tongue which is to us the music
Of enterprise, the family Sunday?

Not in this boat, perhaps, whose twin
Heavy-nippled orange torpedoes
Thunder to the swimmer's touch

And lurch with air-pumped buoyancy
Safely on the benign waters
Of the golfe, a roof to many fish.

For there are still some voyages
And destinies that boats will not
Outlast, for all their jolly rigging.

Except maybe its older brother,
The little tub with the stiff rowlocks
That bobs and circles to the oar.

For look: there it is, still at sea,
Calm in the afternoon, and Ange
Alone there in his crimson cap.

IGUANA DAYS

We have seen this pebble before
Though three feet under. From year
To year it changes position.

The sea dwindles its contours
But not to my brief eye
In a mere decade of watching.

Stone keeps its secrets.
Its smoothness is a ruse
To content us with surface.

At the heart of stone is pure
Concentration, which life
Is foolishly in love with.

We believe that the stillness comes
From its exact possession
Of a truth that is lost to us.

. . . . .

In the Wiener Museum,
The iguana enacts
Such stillness, elbows braced

And leaning forward into
Thought, years of reflection
Shaping its motionless grin.

It reminds us of Sutherland's Maugham,
Though there is not a trace
Of that creative arrogance.

Its skin has become stone,
The brain is a stone, finally
Empty of all anxiety.

To bask like this on stone,
Like stone: a century
Might pass before you move.

So we make our images:
The eternity of the pebble,
The monumental pose.

Out in the street sits Ferdinand
Raimund in the repose
Of his theatrical success.

The boulevards circle the city
As the mind deliberates upon
Its roaring purposes.

It is like the sea's eager
Auditorium, between
The curtains of dusk and dawn

And Raimund is now marble,
Inattentive to applause, finger
Forever marking his chiselled page.

POSITIONS IN BED

Hand sandwich, cold shoulder, glued knees:
There are long times in the night when sleep
Induces some unrelaxing postures.
Settling into them seems sensible:
The lightly-crossed shins, one instep
Upon the other ankle-bone,
The arm across the chest, fingers
Cupped like an epaulette, the chin
Erect on the pillow, as if for shaving.
Or risking the supine snore-prone loll,
The knee crooked at an angle, an arm
Cradling the yearning furrowed brow.
Or striding, striding, taking up
Quite as much of the bed as one dares,
One wrist over the edge of the mattress.
All these are credible positions
Even when we find ourselves
Suddenly, irritatingly awake
And able, indeed positively induced,
To analyse them at leisure, fearing
To move and wake our sleeping partner.

How, then, should we seek our perfect
Oblivion? Much like a crusader?
Ankles crossed and praying hands?
Or coffin-style, perfect repose,
A horizontal sentry-box,
Promptly lying to attention?
The thing about these bodily
Dispositions is their limited
Vareity and likely discomfort.
Really we need to lose an arm,
Acquire a three-way socket for
The ankles, a mattress-cave for the hips.
Consider: to compose the body

Is a necessary preliminary
To the nightly act of its translation.
Perhaps one morning we will find
Ourselves absconded from the body's
Weary roll-call, unreturned
From the wild encounters that we seek
And nothing left of us but posture,
The crumpled relic of restlessness.

BICYCLE

Drifting through my head one morning
At 5 am, some memories
From 1947 or 8.

The lunchtime ritual at Miss 'aunder's,
Corned beef thinly sliced, cold,
With hot dumped mashed potato.

The two bland flavours competing
With their anomalous temperatures
For the ready favours of appetite.

Filing in behind our plates
Already sparely filled, water
In fluted jugs, quarters of bread.

Our uniform was mauve and green.
Miss 'aunder herself throughout the meal
Talked aloud on subjects of interest.

But what was drifting through my head
On such occasions? Was I already
Looking forward to my escape?

To ride precipitously down
The Blackheath vales, almost as steep
As quarries, slithery with pebbles of flint.

The paths scored with runnels dry
Of water, danger to launched bikes
As they slalomed the clumps of thorn.

Later I learned that the heath had many
Plague-pits, and the highwaymen
Once galloped over London's dead.

I tried to think of all the bodies
Needed to fill up one vale
Like a Lord Mayor's pie of whitebait.

I had seen Werner Von Braun
Attempt to re-open one: the crater
Was scattered with the jagged steel

As though a giant had been attacking
Beans, and the pieces were still hot.
There was nothing there, a pit of water.

And a single body lay nearby
Like a secretary asleep on the grass,
With a pram, which someone had set upright.

I had thought this incident somehow
Theoretical or inadequate, though
My bedroom bulb had bounced to the ceiling.

And I remembered the crowds and fires
Of the evening of victory, the shouting,
And the wandering, simply to see more people.

Now in peacetime, in mauve and green,
I listened to Miss 'aunder, doyenne
Of table-talk and mashed potato.

What did she talk about? Not death,
I think, nor the topography
Of death. Nor about bicycles.

WAITING

The little body I was in
Starred on the grass. While all around
The grimed yellow brick of London

Projected its iron balustrades
Into the theatres of unpruned garden,
Stalls of laurel, gods of willow,

With flinty paths on which my cats
Stood unconcerned as usherettes
And the clouds passing like scenery.

Gardens are the soliloquies
Of our agon with the authorial earth,
All morning interrogating worms.

All afternoon crucifying a tree
With an air-pistol, the silvery slugs
Studding the bark like slow typing.

I was still waiting for the scene to open,
Waiting for the downy-jawed girl
From the flat downstairs to come and play.

The lonely tangent of childhood locked
Into its slow ascent, the world
Bathed in the weathers of its future.

TOO LATE

Summer of all seasons in its core
We feel to be wasted. It has passed
Almost unnoticed, like happiness.

How early it began! Earlier
Than we had realised, not too late
It seems, to take it fully to heart.

The welcome of a wood suffused
With bluebells which we never saw,
The mating of thrushes, thickening grass.

These things occurred while we were waiting
For them to occur, and leaves made shade
That still required the sun to prove it.

The year's tennis star is crouched
At the service line of his career.
The ball is dripping from his hand.

The gum of the sycamore is suspended
Like aerial gossamer above
My pile of examination scripts.

We are booked like actors to appear
At the triumphant opening:
The leaves are a superfluity of tickets.

We approach summer like conquerors
Entering a city already ravaged,
Hollow stems and dried blossoms.

Scorched grasses with lines of ants
Like native bearers, spikes and thorns,
The reek of pods and seeded herbs.

The exhalation of the summer,
Its reach and perfect stillness, the sea's
Calm at the close of a sandy path

Bearing a dab of a white sail
Like a sudden excitement, all now
Forgotten, shut from the restless mind.

Now there will be no more of it.
Now pears bomb a vacant flower-bed
And garden wood is damp to the grasp.

Now we are in a mood to expect nothing
But the rich disappointment of the mood itself,
The heavy bending of a plant that is shed

Of its compulsions towards the receiving soil
And whose root now takes a grip of that dank chill
Even as its stalk springs lightly back.

BETRAYAL

The petal on the grass,
The promise lightly made,
The leaf tugged from the branch.

The child and mother, centre
Of their circumference,
Kneel in their daily play.

What is it that we say
At their abandonment?
'He simply walked away.'

He walked away from them
Into the world of his
Peculiar satisfactions

As if in obedience
To the welcomed compulsion
Of self-realisation.

The worst of failure is
To think or talk it into
The light of some advantage

When it might reach fulfilment
By being understood,
Or cease to be a fault.

Is is the bland belief
That we may find it credible
Enough to be forgiven.

'No one understands me . . .'
'It isn't that simple . . .'
The withered leaf.

SONG

Yellow's the stubble of winter,
Yellow's the trumpet of spring,
The yawn of the tulip awakens
A throat that will sing.

The wine is the green of the summer,
The lime is the green of its leaf,
The scents of a season dissemble
The taste of its grief.

And now is a time of no colour,
The stem and the fruit are cut,
The branch is bare at the window
And lips are shut.

FREEZE

Our normally effusive friend
Has nothing to say: he has dried up
Like an actor on a too-long tour.

That grave soliloquy into
The bath, that ready repartee
With the kettle: all utterly forgotten.

Ice-cube wit, lavatory humour:
Not even a splutter of protest.
It's his last gasp, horribly smothered.

His understudy is to hand,
Chattering away to himself
Out there as usual on the hillside,

So I'm off to teach him what I can
In my coat and muffler and grim cap
And a pair of buckets like a milkmaid.

Thank God for Nature when supplies
Fail us. I can write by sunlight
Though it will not bring me Handel.

The birds will have to do, although
In this deep stillness few are forthcoming.
They must be playing away this season.

The sound of my feet on the frozen ground
Reminds me I'd rather be eating biscuits
With the mug of coffee the tap denies me.

First things first, as the Master said,
So I sink and tug one dripping bucket,
Then the other, out of Wilbur

And admire for a moment, in the fall
Between boulders, the shapes of ice
In blebs and shanks and grassy knobs

And the long fingers that play upon
Their secret organ-pipes the quick
Voluntary of the stream.

ASH

At early light the cold is like
A second door. The ash twigs stir
And crack. I hurry with the basket
Along the sheepway from the barn,
Walking taller on yesterday's prints
That are now frozen into moonscape.

It weighs like the dismembered branch
It must contain, and I feel like
A murderer with a guilty suitcase.
It was not I. It was the wind.
And yet the saw is oiled and ready.
Lovers of trees must still keep warm.

GAMES

for Mick

Your boots are here, taller than mine
And with swish buckles, against your return.
Whenever I wear them I have a desire

To run on the spot with little steps
Like a substitute preparing himself,
Or to kick out at foxgloves, wildly.

I have emended the Rules of Cottage Golff
To take account of time's casual
Handling of this collapsing terrain.

Also in expectation the kitchen
Is laid with garage glasses and Jamesons,
And smoke already fills the rafters.

Alfred Tennyson is here, coughing
Over a fag, and counting out
Yellows and greens, and blues and reds.

Browning is shuffling all the packs,
Including the one where the nine of hearts
Is a brown vole from a children's game.

Alfred, soon writing IOUs,
Looks in the dresser for another
Bottle. He speaks extremely slowly.

'Lucky that cigarettes came in
Just as I was thinking of
Dear Ida and her fainting Prince.

They gave the thing a certain lift.'
Robert looks up and motions him
Back to the table: 'Come on, get dealt.'

'I have in mind,' says Alfred, 'an account
Of life as a perpetuity
Of warring graves, a diminishment

Lit only fitfully by eyes
Looking up in uncertain hope
From the pressed latch of the trysting-gate.'

'A hope too far,' Robert replies.
'Surely it is precisely there
That the betrayals proceed unhindered?'

The cards are dealt, and for a time
The world and its violence are redeemed.
By smoke and abstract speculation.

Will you not join us? There is chocolate.
And, after midnight, five-card tricks
To be doubled. Re-doubled. And won.

And from the other room, the drone
Of pipes and swaying strings, wooing
Us insistently with song.

It is the poet Kangarova
With the catch in her voice and her derisive
'Yok, yok, yok, yok.'

She is known only to this hillside
In Wales, and because she sings for me
She will sing freely to all my friends.

And in the morning, if the weather
Allows, there by the door are standing
The rubber shapes of your restless feet.

GRANDFATHER

Now that we have inherited
The titles and ailments consistent
With the dignity claimed by age
We should learn to keep silent
Or to show at most a stoicism
At these unforeseen contradictions.

We shouldn't try to believe
That the failures of the bone-house,
Like appointments or shopping-lists,
Can ever be out of date
Or realistically ignored
Like a route wrongly taken.

For now we find ourselves
Aware of allargandos,
Small aches and impairments
That prove a consciousness,
After all, of its own
Significant events

As well as those that involve
The world outside it. And so
We note, with fond amusement,
Our still being able to run up-
stairs, or the kerb an in-
ch deeper than we expected.

CALLING

There, don't you hear it too?
Something is calling, although
The day is blank and grey.

The eye fastened on nothing,
The ear undistracted
And we with nothing to say.

But still that sense of calling,
Of something seeking attention
Beyond our consciousness.

That voice in voiceless things
When they cease to be themselves,
Losing their choice and purpose,

Joining the indiscriminate
Otherness which surrounds us
At our own times of withdrawal.

It is then that the world calls us
As if to reinterpret
Or to reconfigure.

Whose is this voice? A god's?
Surely not. It seems
To be the voice of duty

That speaks of origins
And of relationships
Between things grown apart.

And I remember the muezzin
Singing every morning
Raptly, as if for himself.

Singing in the dark hour
At a distance, over all,
And yet outside our door.

His practised lilt spoke more
Of the puzzles of night than of
The determinations of morning

As though the light had still
To be charmed into being
And each day a reward.

The voice is much like his,
A commanding meditation
Rising from the blankness

Of a sleeping senselessness,
Thoughtful, improbable,
But stirring us to beauty.

And like his, the voice
Links us for a while
In its reiterations

Then ends abruptly, as if
Distracted by something else
Of no great importance.

DUSK AND DAWN

In Mahabalipuram
We prepared for sleep, careful
Of the scuttling lizards.

When you suddenly woke
In the middle of the night
('We have to catch a taxi!')

It seemed appropriate
To a ready mode of moving
Between our plotted points

And I half believed you, awake
In a room reduced by darkness,
A refinement of uncertainties.

For I realised that the primitive
Air-conditioning had made
Me dream I was on a train.

There is a style of adventuring
And a delight in journeys
Which appeases life's anxieties

And this is their contained model,
Where any circumstance
May be hostile or benign

And all the world's treasures
Are never enough to ransom
An afternoon's heartache.

And I remembered Greece
In 1959
With an untroubled vision

Of our young bodies still walking
Together hand-in-hand
Through the heat and dust

As well, I suppose, they may
In some god's imagination
Even when we are dead.

We had our lives in prospect:
Innocent, wasteful, beautiful,
All that the young must be.

After forty years and more
We are what the old must become:
Resigned, cautious, hopeful.

It might be that we slept
Beneath the moon on Rhodes
And woke in this older land

Where the crickets at dusk
And the stoneworkers at dawn
Make a similar music.

Tapping at first light
In a regular syncopation,
Near, but invisible,

And far, and much further,
Strangely aware of each other,
On the beach, in the town,

And falling in and out
Of mysterious synchrony
That is like the music of marriage.